# The complete candle making recipes for beginners to the expert.

## A Detailed step by step guide to making incredible homemade candle with different fragrance.

By

ANNE  RUSSELL

# Table of Contents

# Introduction

Candles have been around since the beginning of time when early civilizations began using them as a source of light. While we have since advanced and have the modern comfort of that small thing we call electricity, candles remain a favorite thing for many people to have around the home. Many people enjoy lighting candles because of the nice fragrance they offer and peaceful and pleasant ambiance they create. And while they can be used on a daily basis to create a cozy atmosphere, they are nearly a "must have" when setting the scene for a special occasion whether it is a birthday, holiday, intimate cocktail party or romantic dinner. Unfortunately, buying candles can often be a bit pricy (Yankee candles often cost over $20 for a small jar). It is this high appeal and high cost which has lead many people to say "Hey I can make my own homemade candles!" Yes, you can.

Candlemaking can be an easy, fun and even lucrative hobby for those you who have considered the world of homemade candles.

There are so many creative options to experiment with when venturing into homemade candles including colors, scents, containers, molds and various decorative techniques. However, one of the most basic things to consider when getting started is whether there is a particular type of wax you'd like to work with. There are many options, each of which have their own qualities and benefits and different manners of working with. Also keep in mind that different types of wax often have different melting points (the degree at which the wax converts from a solid to a

[1]

liquid). Always make sure you know a particular wax's melting point (more on this to come once we get into homemade candles instructions).

Following are some of they main types of wax you can choose to work with and a bit of information about them:

# Paraffin Wax

The vast majority of candles that people buy are made of paraffin wax. A by-product of crude oil, it's the most common wax used by candle makers mostly because it is relatively inexpensive. Paraffin wax is sold in blocks which often differ in their appearance. There are different grades of paraffin, separated according to their melting points (harder wax has a higher melting point). Soft paraffin wax is recommended for making candles in containers, but not for the creation of molded or carved candles. Medium paraffin wax should only be used for making poured candles and hard paraffin is suitable for carved and molded candles and has a longer burning time compared to its softer counterparts.

# Beeswax

Beeswax is an all-natural, non-toxic waxy substance secreted by bees after they consume honey and is often preferred by people who like natural products. Beeswax candles burn much longer than paraffin candles, but the wax is more expensive as it isn't as readily available as paraffin. Because beeswax is sticky, it is not a good choice for molded candles. You can purchase beeswax in blocks, chunks, beads or sheets. The advantage of using sheets is that they don't have to be melted; they can actually be hand-rolled into candles. For this reason, beeswax sheets can be a wonderful option if you are planning on making your homemade candles with or around children.

Other advantages of beeswax candles include:

- ❖ Naturally sweetly-scented as opposed to artificially-scented
- ❖ Give a soft and beautiful glow that is closest to natural sunlight
- ❖ Because they are all-natural they do not produce toxic by-products and are virtually smokeless when burned

# Gel Wax

Gel wax is made from gelled mineral oils and plastic polymer. It is rather tricky to manage it's melting, so it is not recommended for beginners. However, gel candles have the advantage that because they are usually rubbery and transparent, there are all kinds of possibilities to customize them by putting decorative objects in them such as shells, metal charms, marbles, art glass, pebbles, etc. Because they are highly customizable, they often make wonderful gifts. Gel candles burn about twice as long as a paraffin candle of the same size and provide a stronger light source as well. One important thing to keep in mind with gel wax is that is has a very high melting point (almost 100 degrees hotter than paraffin wax) so you must be very careful when working with gel wax and use a safe and heat resistant container.

# Soy Wax

Another wonderful all natural alternative which is gaining significant popularity are soy candles, which are made from soybeans. Compared with paraffin, soy candles burn cleaner and longer. In addition, soy wax spills are easy to clean-you can simply use soap and hot water rather than harsh chemicals. This also means it's easier to wash your candle making equipment!

Because of their inherently natural nature, soy candles are greatly complemented by essential oils as opposed to synthetic scents and can make great aromatherapy candles. Soy candles serve as an environmentally friendly alternative to paraffin and an economically friendly alternative to beeswax. Another advantage is that because soy wax is a renewable resource and quite popular, it's readily available and easy to find.

# Bee Honey Candle

## Ingredients

1. yellow wax dye
2. 1 pound of wax

[5]

3.  5 – 10 drops honey suckle oil

# Instructions

- ❖ Shave or cut wax into smaller pieces, into a small pan. Heat wax to melt using a double boiler, add in yellow wax candle dye and mix thoroughly, add a few drops of honeysuckle oil and thoroughly stir once more.

- ❖ Taking mold of choice cut a length of wick which will be the same depth as the candle and about two inches extra. Wrap the end of the cut wick around a pencil (or similar) long enough to balance across the mold and allow the wick to trail to the bottom of your mold (how about something giving a floral result).

- ❖ Slowly pour in the melted wax mixture into the well of mold, which should be on a flat surface and held securely to avoid spillage, leaving the wick and its holder (ie pencil) in place.

- ❖ Set aside and allow solidify and cool for least 16 hours or 24 hours for better result.

- ❖ Gently unwind the wick holder (ie pencil) and then trim to a quarter of an inch long a long wick means a bigger flame and a shorter life for your candle

# Banish Bugs Candle

# Ingredients

1. green wax dye

2. 1 pound of wax

3. 5 – 10 drops lime citronella oil

# Instructions

❖ Shave or cut wax into smaller pieces, into a small pan. Heat wax to melt using a double boiler, add yellow wax candle dye and stir thoroughly.

❖ Add a few drops of lime citronella oil and thoroughly stir once more.

❖ Taking mold of choice cut a length of wick which will be the same depth as the candle and about two inches extra. Wrap the end of the cut wick around a pencil (or similar) long enough to balance across the mold and allow the wick to trail to the bottom of your mold (maybe here a ladybug or beetle would be good).

❖ Slowly pour in the melted wax mixture into the well of mold, which should be on a flat surface and held securely to avoid spillage, leaving the wick and its holder (ie pencil) in place.

❖ Set aside and allow solidify and cool for least 16 hours or 24 hours for better result.

❖ Gently unwind the wick holder (ie pencil) and then trim to a qarter of an inch long a long wick means a bigger flame and a shorter life for your candle.

# Calming Candle

# Ingredients

1. 1.1 pound of wax
2. 5 – 10 drops sandalwood oil
3. brown wax dye
4. 5 – 10 drops jasmine oil

# Instructions

❖ Shave or cut wax into smaller pieces, into a small pan. Heat wax to melt using a double boiler, add brown wax candle dye and mix together thoroughly, add a few drops of jasmine oil and sandalwood oil and thoroughly stir once more.

❖ Taking mold of choice cut a length of wick which will be the same depth as the candle and about two inches extra. Wrap the end of the cut wick around a pencil (or similar) long enough to balance across the mold and allow the wick to trail to the bottom of your mold (the tree mix would suit a candle resembling a sturdy tree trunk).

❖ Slowly pour in the melted wax mixture into the well of mold, which should be on a flat surface and held securely to avoid spillage, leaving the wick and its holder (ie pencil) in place.

❖ Set aside and allow to solidify and cool for at least 16 hours or 24 hours for better result. Gently unwind the wick holder (ie pencil) and then trim to a quarter of an inch long a long wick means a bigger flame and a shorter life for your candle.

# Nuture Nature Candle

[11]

# Ingredients

1. Yellow wax dye
2. 1 pound of wax (soy wax works well here)
3. 5 – 10 drops citronella oil

# Instructions

❖ Shave or cut wax into smaller pieces, into a small pan. Heat wax to melt using a double boiler, add in yellow wax candle dye and stit well to mix, add a few drops of citronella oil and thoroughly stir once more.

❖ Taking mold of choice cut a length of wick which will be the same depth as the candle and about two inches extra. Wrap the end of the cut wick around a pencil (or similar) long enough to balance across the mold and allow the wick to trail to the bottom of your mold (perhaps the fruity aroma should be reflected in a candle shaped like a lemon).

❖ Slowly pour in the melted wax mixture into the well of mold, which should be on a flat surface and held securely to avoid spillage, leaving the wick and its holder (ie pencil) in place.

❖ Set aside and allow to solidify and cool for at least 16 hours or 24 hours for a better result.

❖ Gently unwind wick holder (ie pencil) and then trim to a quarter of an inch long a long wick means a bigger flame and a shorter life for your candle.

[12]

# Tropical Beach Party Candle

## Ingredients

1. Yellow wax dye
2. 1 pound of wax
3. 5 – 10 drops coconut fragrance oil

## Instructions

❖ Shave or cut wax into smaller pieces, into a small pan. Heat wax to melt using a double boiler, add in yellow wax candle dye and stir well to mix, add a few drops of coconut oil, thoroughly stir once more

❖ Taking mold of choice cut a length of wick which will be the same depth as the candle and about two inches extra. Wrap the end of the cut wick around a pencil (or similar) long enough to balance across the mold and allow the wick to trail to the bottom of your mold (how about using real shells for an authentic beach flavor).

❖ Slowly pour in the melted wax mixture into the well of mold, which should be on a flat surface and held securely to avoid spillage, leaving the wick and its holder (ie pencil) in place.

❖ Set aside and allow to solidify and cool for at least 16 hours or 24 hours for better result.

❖ Gently unwind wick holder (ie pencil) and then trim to a quarter of an inch long a long wick means a bigger flame and a shorter life for your candle.

# Spicy Nights Candle

# Ingredients

1. brown wax dye

2. 5 – 10 drops ginger fragrance oil

3. 1 pound of wax

# Instructions

❖ Shave or cut wax into smaller pieces, into a small pan. Heat wax to melt using a double boiler, add brown wax candle dye and stir well to mix, add a few drops of ginger fragrance oil, thoroughly stir once more.

❖ Taking mold of choice cut a length of wick which will be the same depth as the candle and about two inches extra. Wrap the end of the cut wick around a pencil (or similar) long enough to balance across the mold and allow the wick to trail to the bottom of your mold (metal molds used to make gingerbread are surely a must here).

❖ Slowly pour in the melted wax mixture into the well of mold, which should be on a flat surface and held securely to avoid spillage, leaving the wick and its holder (ie pencil) in place.

❖ Set aside and allow to solidify and cool for at least 16 hours or 24 hours for a better result.

❖ Gently unwind the wick holder (ie pencil) and then trim to a quarter of an inch long a long wick means a bigg

# Feeling Of The Forest Candle

[17]

# Ingredients

1. 1 pound of wax

2. 5 – 10 drops pinewood fragrance oil

3. green wax dye

# Instructions

❖ Shave or cut wax into smaller pieces, into a small pan. Heat wax to melt using a double boiler, add green wax candle dye and stir well to mix, add in few drops of pinewood fragrance oil, thoroughly stir once more.

❖ Taking mold of choice cut a length of wick which will be the same depth as the candle and about two inches extra. Wrap the end of the cut wick around a pencil (or similar) long enough to balance across the mold and allow the wick to trail to the bottom of your mold (maybe a couple of metal Xmas tree cookie cutters is the best idea).

❖ Slowly pour in the melted wax mixture into the well of mold, which should be on a flat surface and held securely to avoid spillage, leaving the wick and its holder (ie pencil) in place.

❖ Set aside and allow to solidify and cool, for at least 16 hours or 24 hours for a better result.

❖ Gently unwind wick holder (ie pencil) and then trim to a quarter of an inch long a long wick means a bigger flame and a shorter life for your candle.

# Hive Of Inactivity Candle

[19]

# Ingredients

1. 1 pound of wax (clearly beeswax would work well with this relaxing)

2. 5 – 10 drops honey fragrance oil

3. yellow wax dye

# Instructions

❖ Shave or cut wax into smaller pieces, into a small pan. Heat wax to melt using a double boiler, add yellow wax candle dye and stir well to mix, add in few drops of honey fragrance oil, thoroughly stir once more.

❖ Taking mold of choice cut a length of wick which will be the same depth as the candle and about two inches extra. Wrap the end of the cut wick around a pencil (or similar) long enough to balance across the mold and allow the wick to trail to the bottom of your mold (the recipe simply cries out for a beehive-shaped mold).

❖ Slowly pour in the melted wax mixture into the well of mold, which should be on a flat surface and held securely to avoid spillage, leaving the wick and its holder (ie pencil) in place.

❖ Set aside and allow to solidify and cool, for at least 16 hours or 24 hours for better result.

❖ Gently unwind the wick holder (ie pencil) and then trim to a quarter of an inch long a long wick means a bigger flame and a shorter life for your candle.

# Floral Fragrance Candle

# Ingredients

1. blue wax dye

2. 5 – 10 drops rose essence oil

3. 1 pound of wax

# Instructions

❖ Shave or cut wax into smaller pieces, into a small pan. Heat wax to melt using a double boile, add blue wax candle dye and stir well to mix, add in few drops of rose essence oil, thoroughly stir once more.

❖ Taking mold of choice cut a length of wick which will be the same depth as the candle and about two inches extra. Wrap the end of the cut wick around a pencil (or similar) long enough to balance across the mold and allow the wick to trail to the bottom of your mold (another recipe suiting a floral shape, it does not have to be an obvious flower, the aroma does that, the suggestion of a flower is enough).

❖ Slowly pour in the melted wax mixture into the well of mold, which should be on a flat surface and held securely to avoid spillage, leaving the wick and its holder (ie pencil) in place.

❖ Set aside and allow to solidify and cool, for at least 16 hours or 24 hours for a better result.

❖ Gently unwind the wick holder (ie pencil) and then trim to a quarter of an inch long a long wick means a bigger flame and a shorter life for your candle.

# Butterfly Butter Massage Candle

[23]

# Ingredients

1. Yellow wax dye

2. 5 – 10 drops mango butter essential oil

3. 1 pound of wax

# Instructions

❖ Shave or cut wax into smaller pieces, into a small pan. Heat wax to melt using a double boiler, add yellow wax candle dye and stir well to mix, add in few drops of mango butter oil, thoroughly stir once more.

❖ Taking mold of choice cut a length of wick which will be the same depth as the candle and about two inches extra. Wrap the end of the cut wick around a pencil (or similar) long enough to balance across the mold and allow the wick to trail to the bottom of your mold (as the name suggests, this should be a butterfly-shaped mold).

❖ Slowly pour in the melted wax mixture into the well mold, which should be on a flat surface and held securely to avoid spillage, leaving the wick and its holder (ie pencil) in place.

❖ Set aside and allow to solidify and cool, for at least 16 hours or 24 hours for better result.

❖ Gently unwind the wick holder (ie pencil) and then trim to a quarter of an inch long a long wick means a bigger flame and a shorter life for your candle.

[24]

# Summer Meadows Candle

# Ingredients

1. green wax dye

2. 5 – 10 drops clover essential oil 1 pound of wax

# Instructions

❖ Shave or cut wax into smaller pieces, into a small pan. Heat wax to melt using a double boiler, add green wax candle dye and stir well to mix, add in few drops of clover essential oil, thoroughly stir once more.

❖ Take mold of choice cut a length of wick which will be the same depth as the candle and about two inches extra. Wrap the end of the cut wick around a pencil (or similar) long enough to balance across the mold and allow the wick to trail to the bottom of your mold (suggest a dome shape mold reminiscent of the flower of the clover).

❖ Slowly pour in the melted wax mixture into the well of mold, which should be on a flat surface and held securely to avoid spillage, leaving the wick and its holder (ie pencil) in place.

❖ Set aside and allow to solidify and cool, for at least 16 hours or 24 hours for a better result.

❖ Gently unwind wick holder (ie pencil) and then trim to a quarter of an inch long a long wick means a bigger flame and a shorter life for your candle.

# Stars And Stripes Candle

## Ingredients

1. candle glitter

2. 2 pounds wax

3. red wax dye

4. blue wax dye

5. 10 – 15 drops blueberry fragrance oil

## Instructions

❖ Shave or cut wax into smaller pieces, into a small pan. Heat wax to melt using a double boile, add blue wax candle dye and mix thoroughly. Add in few drops of blueberry fragrance oil, thoroughly stir once more.

❖ Taking a mold large enough to create a single candle out of all the wax, cut a length of wick which will be the same depth as the candle and about two inches extra. Wrap the end of the cut wick around a pencil (or similar) long enough to balance across the mold and allow the wick to trail to the bottom of your mold (the recipe is best used when producing a fatter candle).

❖ Allow this to solidify and cool for at least 16 – 24 hours. Prepare next half a pound of wax, adding the blueberry fragrance but omitting dye as this will be the white band.

- Leave until it has cooled and is just beginning to solidify. A quick stir will re melt the crust which is forming and then add to the mold. Leaving it to cool first prevents this layer melting the blue section of candle but melts enough to seal the two layers.

- Allow to solidify and cool for at least 16 hours.

- Prepare last half a pound of wax as above, adding red wax dye and the blueberry fragrance. Allow until it has cooled and is just beginning to solidify. A quick stir will re melt the crust which is forming and then add to the mold. Leaving it to cool first prevents this layer melting the white section of candle but melts enough to seal the two adjoining layers.

- Allow to solidify and cool, at least 16 hours.

- Gently unwind wick holder (ie pencil) and then trim to a quarter of an inch long a long wick means a bigger flame and a shorter life for your candle.

- When set remove from the mold and sprinkle the glitter on to a piece of wax paper. Warming the candle with a hairdryer on a low setting gently roll the candle in the glitter and the effect is complete.

# Typically Tropical Candle

# Ingredients

1. yellow wax dye

2. 1 pound of wax

3. 5 – 10 drops pineapple essential oil

# Instructions

- ❖ Shave or cut wax into smaller pieces, into a small pan. Heat wax to melt using a double boile, add yellow wax candle dye and stir well to mix, add in few drops of pineapple oil, thoroughly stir once more.

- ❖ Take mold of choice cut a length of wick which will be the same depth as the candle and about two inches extra. Wrap the end of the cut wick around a pencil (or similar) long enough to balance across the mold and allow the wick to trail to the bottom of your mold (a pineapple-shaped mold will be ideal).

- ❖ Slowly pour in the melted wax mixture into the well of mold, which should be on a flat surface and held securely to avoid spillage, leaving the wick and its holder (ie pencil) in place.

- ❖ Set aside and allow to solidify and cool, for at least 16 hours or 24 hours for better result.

- ❖ Gently unwind the wick holder (ie pencil) and then trim to a quarter of an inch long a long wick means a bigger flame and a shorter life for your candle.

[31]

# Pampering Pink Pomegranate Candle

# Ingredients

1. Pink wax dye

2. 1 pound of wax

3. 5 – 10 drops of pomegranate essential oil

# Instructions

❖ Shave or cut wax into smaller pieces, into a small pan. Heat wax to melt using a double boile, add pink wax candle dye and stir well to mix, add in few drops of pomegranate essential oil, thoroughly stir together once more.

❖ Taking your mold of choice cut a length of wick which will be the same depth as the candle and about two inches extra. Wrap the end of the cut wick around a pencil (or similar) long enough to balance across the mold and allow the wick to trail to the bottom of your mold (this very feminine recipe is ideal for a night of pampering and luxury, the aroma and the color are pretty, think of a pretty shape which suits you).

❖ Slowly pour in the melted wax mixture into the well of mold, which should be on a flat surface and held securely to avoid spillage, leaving the wick and its holder (ie pencil) in place.

❖ Set aside and allow to solidify and cool for at least 16 hours or 24 hours for a better result.

❖ Gently unwind the wick holder (ie pencil) and then trim to a quarter of an inch long a long wick means a bigger flame and a shorter life for your candle.

[33]

# American Candle

[34]

# Ingredients

1. green wax dye

2. 5 – 10 drops apple essential oil

3. 1 pound of wax

# Instructions

❖ Shave or cut wax into smaller pieces, into a small pan. Heat wax to melt using a double boile, add a little green wax candle dye (you only want a pale green color) and stir well to mix, add in few drops of apple essential oil, thoroughly stir together once more.

❖ Take mold of choice cut a length of wick which will be the same depth as the candle and about two inches extra. Wrap the end of the cut wick around a pencil (or similar) long enough to balance across the mold and allow the wick to trail to the bottom of your mold (the message here is one of 'apple pie' so perhaps a triangular slice shape would be appropriate).

❖ Slowly pour in the melted wax mixture into the well of mold, which should be on a flat surface and held securely to avoid spillage, leaving the wick and its holder (ie pencil) in place.

❖ Set aside and allow to solidify and cool, for at least 16 hours or 24 hours for a better result

❖ Gently unwind the wick holder (ie pencil) and then trim to a quarter of an inch long a long wick means a bigger flame and a shorter life for your candle.

# Thanksgive Candle

# Ingredients

1. orange wax dye

2. 5 – 10 drops pumpkin essential oil

3. 1 pound of wax

# Instructions

❖ Shave or cut wax into smaller pieces, into a small pan. Heat wax to melt using a double boile, add orange wax candle dye and stir well to mix, add in few drops of pumpkin oil, thoroughly stir together once more.

❖ Take mold of choice cut a length of wick which will be the same depth as the candle and about two inches extra. Wrap the end of the cut wick around a pencil (or similar) long enough to balance across the mold and allow the wick to trail to the bottom of your mold (as we are trying to evoke the warm aroma of the Thanksgiving meal, a triangular shape reminiscent of a slice of pumpkin pie seems the most appropriate).

❖ Slowly pour in the melted wax mixture into the well of mold, which should be on a flat surface and held securely to avoid spillage, leaving the wick and its holder (ie pencil) in place.

❖ Set aside and allow to solidify and cool, for at least 16 hours or 24 hours or a better result.

❖ Gently unwind the wick holder (ie pencil) and then trim to a quarter of an inch long a long wick means a bigger flame and a shorter life for your candle.

# Xmas Candle

# Ingredients

1. green wax dye

2. 5 – 10 drops xmas essential oil blend (pine, cloves, berries, cinnamon, nutmeg are usually incorporated in this mix or you could make your own)

3. 1 pound of wax

# Instructions

❖ Shave or cut wax into smaller pieces, into a small pan. Heat wax to melt using a double boile, add green wax candle dye and stir well to mix, add in few drops of Xmas essential oil, thoroughly stir together once more.

❖ Take mold of choice cut a length of wick which will be the same depth as the candle and about two inches extra. Wrap the end of the cut wick around a pencil (or similar) long enough to balance across the mold and allow the wick to trail to the bottom of your mold (this has to be made using a Xmas tree cookie cutter).

❖ Slowly pour in the melted wax mixture into the well of mold, which should be on a flat surface and held securely to avoid spillage, leaving the wick and its holder (ie pencil) in place.

❖ Set aside and allow to solidify and cool, for at least 16 hours or 24 hours for a better result.

❖ Gently unwind the wick holder (ie pencil) and then trim to a quarter of an inch long a long wick means a bigger flame and a shorter life for your candle.

# Cinnaroma Candle

# Ingredients

1. brown wax dye

2. 5 – 10 drops cinnamon essential oil

3. 1 pound of wax

# Instructions

❖ Shave or cut wax into smaller pieces, into a small pan. Heat wax to melt using a double boile, add brown wax candle dye and stir well to mix, add in few drops of cinnamon oil, thoroughly stir together once more.

❖ Take mold of choice cut a length of wick which will be the same depth as the candle and about two inches extra. Wrap the end of the cut wick around a pencil (or similar) long enough to balance across the mold and allow the wick to trail to the bottom of your mold (the recipe is an aid to relaxation, perhaps while in the bath so perhaps find something which fits with the bath tub).

❖ Slowly pour in the melted wax mixture into the well of mold, which should be on a flat surface and held securely to avoid spillage, leaving the wick and its holder (ie pencil) in place.

❖ Set aside and allow to solidify and cool, for at least 16 hours or 24 hours for a better result.

❖ Gently unwind the wick holder (ie pencil) and then trim to a quarter of an inch long a long wick means a bigger flame and a shorter life for your candle.

[41]

# Win And Dine Candle

[42]

# Ingredients

1. red wax dye

2. 5 – 10 drops wine scented oil

3. 1 pound of wax

# Instructions

❖ Shave or cut wax into smaller pieces, into a small pan. Heat wax to melt using a double boile, add red wax candle dye and stir well to mix, add in few drops of wine oil and stir in thoroughly once again.

❖ Take mold of choice cut a length of wick which will be the same depth as the candle and about two inches extra. Wrap the end of the cut wick around a pencil (or similar) long enough to balance across the mold and allow the wick to trail to the bottom of your mold (a standard candle shape would be appropriate, the effect would be perfect if used with an old wine bottle as a holder).

❖ Slowly pour in the melted wax mixture into the well of mold, which should be on a flat surface and held securely to avoid spillage, leaving the wick and its holder (ie pencil) in place.

❖ Set aside and allow to solidify and cool, for least 16 hours or 24 hours for better result.

❖ Gently unwind the wick holder (ie pencil) and then trim to aquarter of an inch long a long wick means a bigger flame and a shorter life for your candle.

[43]

# Mind And Meditation Candle

# Ingredients

1. 1 pound of wax (this does work well with soy wax)

2. 5 – 10 drops of frankincense essential oil

# Instructions

❖ Shave or cut wax into smaller pieces, into a small pan. Heat wax to melt using a double boile, add in few drops of frankincense oil, thoroughly stir together. Take mold of choice cut a length of wick which will be the same depth as the candle and about two inches extra. Wrap the end of the cut wick around a pencil (or similar) long enough to balance across the mold and allow the wick to trail to the bottom of your mold (the simplicity and longevity of the candle would makes this an ideal recipe for a mason jar).

❖ Slowly pour in the melted wax mixture into the well of mold, which should be on a flat surface and held securely to avoid spillage, leaving the wick and its holder (ie pencil) in place.

❖ Set aside and allow to solidify and cool, for at least 16 hours or 24 hours for a better result

❖ Gently unwind the wick holder (ie pencil) and then trim to a quarter of an inch long a long wick means a bigger flame and a shorter life for your candle.

# Herbal Treatment Candle

[46]

# Ingredients

1. 1 pound of wax

2. sprinkling of dried herbs

3. pink wax dye

# Instructions

❖ Shave or cut wax into smaller pieces, into a small pan. Heat wax to melt using a double boile, add pink wax candle dye and stir well to mix, add dried herbs a little at a time, thoroughly stir together.

❖ Take mold of choice cut a length of wick which will be the same depth as the candle and about two inches extra. Wrap the end of the cut wick around a pencil (or similar) long enough to balance across the mold and allow the wick to trail to the bottom of your mold (this is another candle which would fit well in a mason jar).

❖ Slowly pour in the melted wax mixture into the well mold, which should be on a flat surface and held securely to avoid spillage, leaving the wick and its holder (ie pencil) in place.

❖ Set aside and allow to solidify and cool, for at least 16 hours or 24 hours for a better result.

❖ Gently unwind the wick holder (ie pencil) and then trim to a quarter of an inch long a long wick means a bigger flame and a shorter life for your candle.

# Cherry Blossom Candle

# Ingredients

1. 1 pound of wax

2. 5 – 10 drops of cherry blossom essential oil

3. pink wax dye

# Instructions

❖ Shave or cut wax into smaller pieces, into a small pan. Heat wax to melt using a double boile, add pink wax candle dye and stir well to mix, add in few drops of cherry blossom essential oil, thoroughly stir together.

❖ Take mold of choice cut a length of wick which will be the same depth as the candle and about two inches extra. Wrap the end of the cut wick around a pencil (or similar) long enough to balance across the mold and allow the wick to trail to the bottom of your mold (the recipe simply cries out for a cherry-shaped mold with the wick, and thus the flame, representing the stalk).

❖ Slowly pour in the melted wax mixture into the well of mold, which should be on a flat surface and held securely to avoid spillage, leaving the wick and its holder (ie pencil) in place.

❖ Set aside and allow to solidify and cool, for at least 16 hours or 24 hours for a better result.

❖ Gently unwind the wick holder (ie pencil) and then trim to a quarter of an inch long a long wick means a bigger flame and a shorter life for your candle.

[49]

# Cup Cake Candle

[50]

# Ingredients

1. 1 pound of wax

2. 5 – 10 drops apple essential oil powdered cinnamon

3. yellow wax dye

# Instructions

❖ Shave or cut wax into smaller pieces, into a small pan. Heat wax to melt using a double boile, add yellow wax candle dye and stir well to mix , add in few drops of apple essential oil and thoroughly stir togrther, add powdered cinnamon and stir well to mix thoroughly.

❖ Take mold of choice cut a length of wick which will be the same depth as the candle and about two inches extra. Wrap the end of the cut wick around a pencil (or similar) long enough to balance across the mold and allow the wick to trail to the bottom of your mold (those reusable cupcake containers are ideal as you end up with a cupcake shape).

❖ Slowly pour in the melted wax mixture into the well of mold, which should be on a flat surface and held securely to avoid spillage, leaving the wick and its holder (ie pencil) in place.

❖ Set aside and allow to solidify and cool, for least 16 hours or 24 hours for a better result.

❖ Gently unwind the wick holder (ie pencil) and then trim to a quarter of an inch long a long wick means a bigger flame and a shorter life for your candle.

# Apple Dumpling Candle

[52]

# Ingredients

1. 100 candle wicks

2. 1 slab joy wax

3. 10 pounds pillar of bliss wax

4. caramel color blocks dye

5. apple dumpling fragrance oil

6. cream color blocks dye

7. pouring pot

8. 4 loaf molds, silicone soap mold

9. thermometer

# Instructions

❖ Weigh 120g pillar of bliss candle wax out. Heat wax to melt using a double boile, add in small amount of a caramel color block. Use less than a gram of the color block and want the color to be the color of actual caramel. Stir well to incorporate the colorant. You can test your color by using a spoon to place a small amount of wax on a white paper plate. You well see the true color of the wax, once set, If needed, adjust the color block.

❖ Add 12 g apple dumpling fragrance oil. Thoroughly stir altogether for once.

❖ Pour candle wax into each well of the silicone four loaf mold. We will be cutting this wax into chunks in a later step. Another option is to pour it into a wax paper lined baking pan. Allow the wax to setup, but still be warm to the touch.

❖ Once wax has setup, remove it from the mold. Then, use a knife to cut the wax into square pieces. When you are finished they will look like caramel candies. Set these pieces aside, for now.

❖ Weigh 300g joy wax and melt using a double boiler, add a very small amount of a cream color block, use less than a gram, add 30g apple dumpling fragrance oil. Stir well to incorporate the fragrance oil, add wicks to the jar, adhering them with hot glue. You want to make sure that your wick tabs are centered and evenly placed in the jar.

❖ Pour melted wax into the candle jar. Then, drop your caramel colored cubes gently into the jar. Make sure you keep the wicks straight and centered as you are doing this. Allow your candle to fully setup before trimming the wicks and allowing the candle to cure. for least 16 hours or 24 hours for a better result.

# Aromatherapy Massage Candle

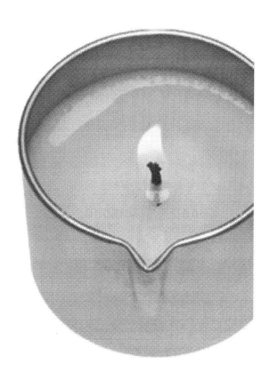

# Ingredients

1. 2 teaspoons avocado oil

2. 2.7 oz eco soya soy wax

3. 1 teaspoon shea butter

4. 20 drops choice of essential oils

# Instructions

❖ Set the jar with candle wick and working space

❖ Heat soy wax and avocado oil together to melt, by using a double boile, stir mixture together, remove from heat and set aside for 5 seconds, add Shea butter to the warm wax and oil mixture stir gently to make sure all the ingredients are blended.

❖ Allow mixture to cool for few minutes while stirring, and have your essential oil ready. The reason the essential oils are added right before pouring, is because they are heat sensitive and evaporate if the wax is still too hot.

❖ Add the essential oils and allow another one or two minutes to blend the whole mixture, before pouring it into the glass jar.

❖ Allow candle to sit overnight.

# Beeswax Candle

[57]

# Ingredients

1. 12 oz. organic palm oil and shortening

2. 12 oz. beeswax, roughly chopped

3. mason jars (I filled 4 half pint jars with this recipe)

4. square braided cotton wick

# Instructions

❖ Collect 12 oz. of beeswax in your large glass measuring cup. Place measuring cup into a pan filled with a few inches of water. Melt beeswax over medium heat. (Do not heat your over high heat, it could ignite.)

❖ While beeswax is melting, cut a taller wicks that will be few inches taller than the jars. Once beeswax begins melting you can carefully dip one cut wick in the wax. After dipping, carefully lay the wick on a sheet of newspaper, holding one end with your fingers, and straightening it out by holding the other end down with a skewer and gently pulling it. Repeat with all the wicks. Allow wicks to dry.

❖ Add palm oil to mostly melted beeswax and stir while it finishes melting. When beeswax and palm oil mixture melts, stir carefully with a skewer. Pour about ½ inch of hot wax into the bottom of one jar, then immediately place a wick into the center of the jar so it just touches the bottom. Hold wick in place gently until wax hardens enough for the wick to stand on its own. Set aside allow solidify completely. Repeat this step with all your jars.

❖ Rest a skewer on top of each jar, gently wrap the wick around the skewer, and make sure it is positioned straight. With wicks secured, finish pouring hot wax into each jar, and leave headspace at the top. Set aside to cool and solidify completely for about 12 – 24 hours.

❖ Cut wicks, leaving them ¼ – ½ inch long. Light and enjoy your beautiful new candles.

# Banana Nut bread Candle

[60]

# Ingredients

1. candle wick

2. mason jar

3. wooden skewer

# Instructions

❖ Collect wax flakes into a jar, make is fill up, heat to melt wax over a medium low heat setting in your oven, placing jar on a center rack, or by placing the jar in the microwave and heating it in short intervals. As wax melts add more flakes and melt, repeating this process until the jar is full of melted wax.

❖ Carefully remove jar of melted wax from the heat source using oven mitts and place on a heat resistant surface. Add fragrance oil to the melted wax using a pipette. Typically for this size candle, I add about 8 – 10 pipettes of fragrance oil (also depending on the potency of the fragrance oil I'm using).

❖ Position the wick in the center of the candle (with the metal disc touching the bottom of the jar) and fold over the wooden skewer to support the placement while the wax hardens. Allow the candle to cool and solidify completely, for about 12 – 24 hours.

❖ Carefully light and enjoy your candle.

# Valentine's Day Candle

[62]

# Ingredients

1. glass jar

2. candle wax (I used advanced soy)

3. candle wick

4. corn syrup

5. strawberry milkshake fragrance oil

6. pink and red heart sprinkles

7. wick stickems, glue dots, or hot glue

# Instructions

❖ Use a pastry brush, coat inside of the jar and immediately sprinkle the hearts onto the syrup. Work in small sections until the entire jar is coated and covered with the hearts. Allow the corn syrup to dry completely before moving on (you can pop the jar in the refrigerator to speed up the process).

❖ Prepare wick by sticking the wick stick ems (or glue dots or a little hot glue) to the metal tab. Press the tab firmly to the bottom of the jar, in the center.

# The wax.

❖ We need double boiler, the amount of wax flakes that your jar holds. This is because as the wax melts, the liquid amount will be half of the dry amount. Be sure to measure this out before prepping the jar.

❖ . Heat wax to melt in a microwave safe bowl or measuring cup (a spout really helps for clean pouring) or until a smooth liquid is achieved.

❖ Remove from heat and allow to cool for few minutes, add fragrance to your melted wax. Note: we will need 1 ounce of fragrance oil for every 1 pound of candle wax. This will give you a nice burning scent.

❖ Carefully pour wax into the prepared jar. Set aside to solidify and cool, for about 12 – 24 hours.

❖ While candle cools you will need to center and anchor the wick. This can be done with a wick clip, a straw, a skewer or anything longer than the jar opening.

# Coffee Cup Candle

[65]

## Ingredients

1. 16 oz mug

2. nature's oil creamy root beer float fragrance oil

3. wick

4. nature's oil golden wax akosoy

5. whole coffee beans (i used vanilla beans)

## Instructions

❖ Put candle wick in the center of a clean mug. Simply by placing wick in center of the mug and prop up using pencils or skewers along with tape.

❖ Heat wax to melt by using microwave safe bowl, begin melting the wax flakes. Start at 35 seconds intervals. For best results, only do a cup or two at a time. Re melt if needed, only at 10 seconds intervals or until you hear the wax my pop. You can also use the double boiler method if you prefer. Just make sure to stir every few minutes.

❖ Add 5 drops and shakes of nature's oil creamy root beer float fragrance oil and ½ cup of whole coffee beans. I used vanilla beans. Stir well to mix and incorporate together and smells amazing.

❖ Slowly pour the hot wax mixture into the mug, avoiding the centered wick. Det aside for 24 hours to solidify before using.

❖ Trim the wick, light and enjoy your new coffee candle

[66]

# Chai Spiced Fall Candle

[67]

# Ingredients

1. 14 – 15 ounces soy wax flakes per candle
2. ½ teaspoon ground ginger
3. 2 candle wicks
4. ½ teaspoon allspice
5. ½ teaspoon cinnamon
6. ½ teaspoon cardamom
7. ½ teaspoon nutmeg
8. 2 8- ounce jar
9. chopsticks or skewers
10. an old pan or clean can for melting wax

# Instructions

❖ Heat wax to melt by placing wax flakes in a double boiler or large glass measuring cup in the microwave.

❖ Dip the end of the candle wicks into the melted wax and adhere to the center of the bottom of the jars. Wrap the wicks around chopsticks or skewers set over the top of the jar to keep the wicks centered.

❖ Once wax has almost melted, remove from heat and stir to finish melting. Add the spices and stir well. (Some will sink to the bottom of the jar.)

❖ Pour the wax into the prepared jars, leaving a little space at the top. Allow to solidify and cool completely, for about 12 – 24 hours.

❖ Trim the wick to desired length and use or give as a gift.

# Pink Mason Jar Candle

[70]

# Ingredients

1. soy wax

2. mason jars

3. mod podge

4. wicks

5. red food coloring

# Instructions

- ❖ Collect and mix 1 tablespoon gloss Mod Podge with ½ tablespoon water in a small cup, add 1 drop red food coloring and mix together. If you want a darker color, add food coloring one drop at a time. When you have a color you like, pour the mixture into the jar and swirl it around until the inside is completely covered.

- ❖ Pour out any excess liquid and allow jars to dry for at least 45 minutes. Then bake at 225OF for an hour. Above is what the jar will look like once baked.

- ❖ After the jars have cooled, slowly melt the soy wax chips using a double broiler and secure the wick to the bottom of the jar. Once the wax is completely melted add essential oil scent and stir. Then pour into the jar and allow it sit until the wax solidify. Trim wick if needed.

# Natural Wax Candle With Essential Oils

[72]

# Ingredients

1. beeswax or carnauba wax

2. essential oils

3. butter, oil, fat of choice

4. wicks

5. glass containers

# Instructions

❖ Melte beeswax, dip a wick end into the melted wax (only works for beeswax) and place in the center of your container. Press into the bottom of the container (use a utensil for pressure if needed, not your bare fingers). The beeswax will solidify and hold your wick in place. This method does not work for carnauba wax. You can secure the wick end with a piece of tape, or pour a bottom layer of wax to cover the wick end and allow to cool while you hold the wick in place.

❖ Suspend wick in the middle of the container by wrapping the excess length of wick around a pencil or skewer and balancing that horizontally across the jar opening.

❖ Add essential oils while the melted wax blend is still on the heat source, right before you pour into your candle containers. Stir quick to incorporate all essential oils that has been added, but do not heat again.

❖ Pour wax into containers, leaving roughly ½ inch of room at the top. Leave boiler insert or measuring cup in the heated water while your candles solidify.

[73]

❖ Once they appear to be solid, this will take 30 – 60 minutes, you will notice that some candles have caved in slightly on the top. You can now top them off with the remaining wax, leaving ¼ inch of room at the top.

❖ Keep aside solidify and cool completely overnight. remove wick holders and snip wicks to ½ inch.

❖ Light and enjoy.

# Homemade Scented Candle

## Ingredients

1. 2kg soy wax or paraffin

2. scented or essential oils or mica or candle powders in various colours (optional the amount you'll need depends on the desired colour, so start with ½ teaspoon and go from there)

3. double boiler (or use a heatproof bowl and a saucepan)

4. thermometer

5. candle moulds (for example small glass jars, tins and pots)

6. spray oil

7. wicks

8. hairdryer

## Instructions

❖ Begin by grating or chopping your wax or paraffin. The smaller you chop it, the quicker it will melt. If you are using a double boiler, get it set up. If you don't have one, boil some water in a large saucepan, then set heatproof bowl on top of the saucepan. Add the wax to the top of the boiler or the bowl and leave to melt, stirring every so often. Use a thermometer to ensure the temperature of the wax does not exceed 90°C.

❖ Once the wax has melted, add your desired oil or combination of oils (for a 250ml-sized candle, about 30ml of oil is ample) and powder for colour, if you wish. I would do this over the heat, very quickly, so that the colouring agent combines easily. Remove from the heat once everything has been added and mixed so that the colour and oil are distributed evenly. Set aside and quickly prep your mould.

❖ If you're using a temporary mould, spray it with a little oil for easy removal. Next, insert the wick by tying the wick to a pencil and sitting it horizontally across the top of the mould so that the wick hangs vertically. Pour in the wax to about 2cm from the top. The candle sometimes shrinks in the centre, so you can add a little more wax if needed. Use a hair dryer to dispel any air bubbles or divots, and smooth the top.

❖ Cut off the wick and leave the candle for at least 24 hours before removing from the mould or lighting it if using a permanent mould.

# Crack Candle

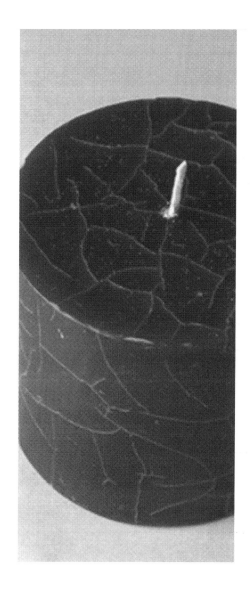

[78]

# Ingredients

1. paraffin wax
2. raw wick
3. wick holder bar or skewer
4. 2 4 lb. pouring pitchers or large buckets
5. fragrance oil (optional)
6. candle dye (optional)
7. scale (recommended)

# Instructions

❖ Melt wax in a double boiler. While the wax is melting, prepare your candle mold by threading the wick through the wick hole, securing at the bottom with a wick screw and covering with mold sealer, and securing the wick at the top with a wick holder bar or skewer

❖ Once wax is melted, add your fragrance oil and candle dye if desired, and mix together thoroughly.

❖ Pour wax into the mold and allow to cool. Be sure to leave a small amount of wax for the second pour

[79]

❖ Poke relief holes in the wax as it cools to prevent air bubbles or warping as the wax shrinks. When the first pour has cooled to room temperature, re melt the left over wax and fill in the sink hole. Allow to cool completely

❖ When the candle is completely cool, remove the mold sealer, wick screw, and wick holder bar and gently remove the candle from the mold. Do not trim the wick yet, as you will need it to hold the candle for the next step

❖ Fill one pitcher or bucket with very hot (but not boiling) water, and the other with very cold water. You can add ice to make it colder if you wish. The colder the water, the better the cracking effect should be. Quickly and smoothly dip the entire candle into the hot water first

❖ Quickly and smoothly dip the entire candle immediately into the cold water. Repeat this process several times, then set the candle on a paper towel to dry off. You may not see the cracks appear right away, but they should appear over time. If you do not see any cracks by the next day, re heat the water and try again.

❖ When you are satisfied with the candle's finished appearance, trim the wick on the bottom to be level with the wax, and trim on the top to about ¼ inch, enjoy.

# Ice Candle

[81]

# Ingredients

1. ice capade fragrance oil

2. 10 pounds pillar of bliss wax

3. 1 oz. purple spectrum liquid candle dye

4. candle wick

5. round pillar candle molds

6. thermometer

7. pouring pot

# Instructions

❖ Melt 1 pound of pillar of bliss wax to 195 degrees, and add Purple Liquid candle dye. Drop melted wax temperature to 180 degrees and add 1 ounce of Ice capade fragrance oil.

❖ Fill mold with crushed ice. You want the ice to be about ¾ inch from the top. Leave a little bit of space at the top to ensure the wax will completely cover the ice.

❖ Pour wax over the ice, allow wax to cool and the ice to melt completely. Once cooled turn the mold upside down over the sink and pour out the melted ice.

❖ Gently, remove the candle from the mold. Please note your candle will be very fragile. Trim wick to ¼ inch. Do not light the candle for about 5 days. To ensure it is completely dry.

[82]

# Christmas Coffee Wax Tarts Candle

[83]

# Ingredients

1. 10 pounds pillar of bliss wax

2. snickerdoodle cookies fragrance oil

3. french vanilla coffee fragrance oil

4. 12 mini muffins silicone soap mold

5. 1oz. brown spectrum liquid candle dye

6. 1oz. black spectrum liquid candle dye

7. pouring pot

8. thermometer

# Instructions

❖ Collect 345g pillar of bliss candle wax for this layer. Use a double boiler to melt tart wax. Once the temperature reaches 195OF, add 3 drops brown candle colorant and 2 drops black candle dye. Stir to fully incorporate the colorant. Allow temperature of the wax to drops to about 180OF, add 41g french vanilla coffee fragrance oil. Stir the wax to fully incorporate your fragrance oil. Fill each cavity a little over halfway full. Then, allow this layer to setup.

❖ Prepare the white portion of the wax melt. Again, we will use a double boiler to melt the wax. This time melt 285 grams of the pillar wax.

❖ When temperature reaches 180OF, add 34g snickerdoodle cookie fragrance oil. Stir once to incorporate the scent. This wax will be poured directly on top of your previous layer. You want the temperature to drop to about 150OF, it so you do not melt the previous layer. So, at this temperature, fill the remaining portions of each cavity. Then, place whole coffee beans on top and allow them to finish setting up.

❖ Once you have allowed your coffee wax melts to cure for a couple of days they are ready to use. Simply place a wax melt in your wax burner and enjoy.

# Christmas Wreath Fire Starters Candle

[86]

# Ingredients

1. 100 candle wicks

2. 10 pounds pillar of bliss wax

3. juniper berries whole

4. christmas wreath type fragrance oil

5. nettle leaf cut and sifted

6. 6 cavity muffin silicone soap mold

7. pouring pot

8. thermometer

# Instructions

❖ Collect and melt 1090g of pillar of bliss wax using a double boiler. While you are waiting, line each cavity of the silicone muffin mold.

❖ Fill each mold with Nettle Leaf Cut and Sifted and Juniper Berries. You want to fill the mold about ¾ of the way full. Cut each wick into 3 equal pieces. You can also use any wick trimming you may have from other projects.

❖ Once wax reaches 180 degrees, add 109g Christmas Wreath Type Fragrance Oil. Mix well. Fill each cavity of the muffin mold with the melted Pillar of Bliss.

❖ Once wax begins to setup, place a wick in the center.

❖ Finally, place nettle leaf around the edges, leaving a circle in the middle. This will create a wreath look. Place the juniper berries to decorate the "wreath. Your Christmas Wreath Fire Starters are now ready to use. Enjoy

# Blueberry Muffin Candle

# Ingredients

1. 10 lbs gel wax

2. beer fragrance oil

3. 1oz. yellow spectrum liquid candle dye

4. 100 candle wicks

5. 1oz. brown spectrum liquid candle dye

6. thermometer

# Instructions

❖ Prepare the wax

❖ Melt 405g of gel wax, using double boiler over medium low heat, Keep an eye on the gel wax as it melts. You will notice that the consistency of the gel wax will become like a thick syrup. Do not allow the temperature of the gel wax to reach 230 degrees or higher. Use your thermometer to monitor this.

❖ Once the gel wax is in a liquid like state, add 1 drop spectrum yellow candle dye, stir well. stick the tip of a toothpick into the Spectrum Brown Candle Dye, then dip the toothpick into the wax. Stir again.

❖ Preparing the Beer Mug

❖ Use a hot glue gun, center and stick your wick to the bottom of the beer mug. Scent gel wax, collect 41g Beer fragrance oil. Remove your gel wax from the heat source and add

[90]

the fragrance. Stir once. Although some bubbles are okay, if you stir too much, or too quickly your gel wax will have too many bubbles.  If this occurs, set it back into the heat source and wait the bubbles out.

❖ Pour gently into the beer mug.  You will want to do this slowly. Straighten your wick and set the candle mug aside to solidify.

❖ Prepare the Foam Topping:

❖ Collect and melt 160g of soy wax, using the double broiler method. Once the soy wax is in a liquid state, remove it from the heat source and add 16g beer fragrance.  Stir.

❖ Pour your scented wax into a mixing bowl and allow to set up slightly.  Next, grab your hand held mixer and begin to mix it.  You will notice as air is incorporated that the wax will become fluffy.  Once the wax has cooled, thickened, and been whipped, begin scooping it into the top of the candle mug.  Continue this until the mug is filled, and has whipped foam wax peaking out of the candle mug.  Allow this to set up. It is now ready to burn.  Simply trim your candle, light, and enjoy.

# Bug Repelling Candle

# Ingredients

1. 1oz. green spectrum liquid candle dye

2. 10 lbs gel wax

3. lime citronella fragrance oil

4. 100 wicks zinc core candle wicks

5. beeswax white pastilles

6. 1oz. yellow  spectrum liquid candle dye

7. pouring pot

8. thermometer

# Instructions

❖ Making the Embeds

❖ Collect 50g beeswax, and melt using double boiler stir occasionally as it melts. Once all beeswax is liquid, add 1 drop spectrum yellow candle dye and stir. Place pouring pot back into the heat source.

❖ Collect 4g lime citronella fragrance oil. Add to the melted beeswax and quickly stir well to incorporate.

❖ Once scented, pour wax into the mini lemon lime mold.  Allow the mold to set up enough to be moved.  Then, place the mold into the freezer.

[93]

❖ Again, use double boiler method, melt another 50g beeswax. Once melted add 1 drop spectrum green candle dye and stir. Once the color is mixed in, place the beeswax back into the heat source.

❖ Remove mold from the freezer. Flip mold upside down and using your thumbs, gently ease the lime slices out of the mold. Set all embeds aside.

❖ Collect 4g lime citronella fragrance oil, add fragrance to the melted beeswax on the stove. Stir well to incorporate, then carefully pour this wax into the lime mold.

❖ When lime slices are hard enough to be moved, carefully place the mold back into the freezer. Allow to set up.

❖ Collect 500g gel wax and melt the gel wax down using the double boiler method. As the gel wax melts, it will be very similar in consistency to a thick syrup. Monitor the gel wax and stir it occasionally.

❖ Remove the lime mold from the freezer and carefully remove the embeds. center and secure your wicks to the bottom of the apothecary jar.

❖ Once your wicks are in place, start placing the lemon embed slices around your candle jar. Press firmly to adhere the embed in place. Once all of the lemon embeds are stuck to the jar, leave a small amount of open area before aligning a lime embed on top. Repeat for each lemon slice.

❖ When the gel wax is all melted, place 1 toothpick tip of spectrum yellow candle Dye and 1 toothpick tip of Spectrum Green Candle Dye into the wax. Stir to incorporate. Finally,

[94]

add 40g lime citronella fragrance to the wax and stir. Place thermometer into the gel wax. Use mixing spoon to keep stir the wax slowly.

- ❖ When gel wax temperature reaches 165OF, slowly pour

# Massage Candle

# Ingredients

1. 108g cocoa butter deodorized
2. 112g shea butter
3. 116g coconut oil
4. 120g soy wax
5. 56g mango butter
6. 26g fragrance oil

# Instructions

❖ Collect all soy wax, cocoa butter, coconut oil 76, shea butter and mango butter, using double boiler to melt. Place over low heat setting and stir occasionally.

❖ In your mixing bowl, max 26g fragrance oil. Set aside.

❖ Once all the ingredients have melted over medium heat, remove from heat and gently stir.

❖ Pour mixture into your mixing bowl that contains the fragrance oil. Use a spatula to ease all of the mixture out. Once again, give a gentle stir to incorporate the fragrance oil throughout the ingredients.

❖ Lay all 4 of your tin cans on a flat surface where they will not be in the way. Once the mixture is poured into these tins, they can not be moved until they are set up.

❖ Pour mixture into your tins. Let mixture set up slightly, then straighten your wick and gently ease it into the tin. Repeat for remaining 3 massage candles.

❖ Allow candles to completely solidify. Then trim your wicks and lid the tins. Once candles are compl completely, they are now ready to use.

# Valentines Day Cupcake Candle

[99]

# Ingredients

1. 10 pounds pillar of bliss wax
2. color blocks dye
3. heart cupcakes silicone soap mold
4. votive candle wick pin
5. 1 slab joy wax
6. cinnamon yum yums fragrance oil
7. 100 wicks candle wicks
8. pouring pot
9. thermometer

# Instructions

## Prepare The Base

❖ Collect 230g pillar of bliss wax. Heat and melt wax to 195OC using the double boiler. While waiting, prepare your molds. You will need 3 of the silicone heart cupcakes molds and 3 wick pins. place one wick pin in the center of each mold.

❖ Add a small amount of your red color block to the melted wax, you will just need a few shavings to achieve a light pink color. Stir well.

[100]

- Allow temperature to drop to 180 degrees. Add 23g cinnamon yum yums fragrance oil, mix well to incorporate the fragrance into the wax.

- pour wax into the molds, filling each mold completely. Allow this portion to setup.

- You will notice you have a bit of wax left over, this will be used for your embeds. Add a couple more shavings of the red color block to the leftover wax. Stir well and be sure the color block is fully incorporated. If want to achieve a red color for the embeds. With wax at a low temperature, pour the wax into the love hearts embed mold. Fill the 3 cavities. Allow embeds to solidify before removing them from the molds.

## Prepare The Frosting

- Melt 140g joy wax to 200 degrees, using a double boiler. Once wax has cooled to 175 degrees, add 14g cinnamon yum yums fragrance oil. stir thoroughly.

- Begin whipping the frosting. Continue to whip as it cools. As it cools and thickens you will notice that it will take on a frosting consistency.

- Carefully, place the wax frosting on top of the candle base. Make sure you do not cover the wick pin completely with wax, but get as close to the top as you can.

- Decorate your candle, add sprinkles and add one of the Love Hearts wax embeds. Once your candle is fully setup, remove it from the mold.

- Carefully, remove the wick pin. Thread 10 wick through the hole left by the wick pin. Trim wick back to ¼ inch before use. Enjoy.

# Witches Brew Candle

## Ingredients

1. 1 oz. black spectrum liquid candle dye

2. 1 case joy wax

3. 1 oz. purple spectrum liquid candle dye

4. 10 pounds pillar of bliss wax

5. witches brew fragrance oil

6. 100 wicks candle

7. pouring pot

8. thermometer

## Instructions

❖ Prepare witch hat. Melt 1 ounce of pillar of bliss candle wax, using double boiler. Once melted, add 2 drops black liquid candle dye. Then, add 0.1 ounces witches brew fragrance oil. Stir well to incorporate the ingredients. Pour wax into the witch hat mold. Once setup, remove it from the mold and set it aside. We will come back to it.

❖ Prepare your candle jar. Adhere 12 candle wicks to the bottom of your candle jar using a hot glue gun.

❖ Prepare the layers. First, prepare a layer of purple wax. Collect and melt 2 ounces candle wax. Once melted, add 0.2g witches brew fragrance oil and 2 drops spectrum purple candle dye. Stir well to incorporate the ingredients. Pour wax into the bottom of the candle jar slowly. Allow this layer to setup before moving to the next step.

❖ Prepare a black layer. Collect 2 ounces joy wax and melt wax and add 0.2 ounces witches brew fragrance oil and 4 drops of the black liquid candle dye. Stir well to incorporate finally, pour melted wax directly on top of the purple layer and allow it to setup.

❖ Repeat steps 3 and 4 preparing a purple layer, then a black layer, then, another purple layer and a final black layer. You will have a total of six layers.

❖ Finally, prepare your whipped topping. Melt 3 ounces of Joy wax, once melted, add 0.3 ounces witches brew fragrance oil and 1 drop purple liquid candle dye. Stir well.

❖ Allow wax to begin to thicken, at this point begin whipping the candle wax until you have a whipped frosting type look. Place wax on top of your candle and add your witch hat embed you prepared earlier. Finally, use a pencil to curl the wicks. Let your candle cure for a few days before using or selling it. Trim the wicks back to ¼ inch before burning it.

❖ Your witches brew candle is now ready to use. Enjoy.

# Rainbow Candle

# Ingredients

1. 10 pounds pillar of bliss wax
2. rainbow fragrance oil
3. 1 oz. red spectrum liquid candle dye
4. 1 oz. yellow spectrum liquid candle dye
5. 1 oz. orange spectrum liquid candle dye
6. 1 oz. purple spectrum liquid candle dye
7. 1 oz. blue spectrum liquid candle dye
8. 1oz. green spectrum liquid candle dye
9. 100 wicks candle
10. 16 oz. glass apothecary jar
11. ziplock bags for mixing colored wax
12. hot glue gun

# Instructions

❖ Use a hot glue gun, attach 2 wicks to the bottom of your apothecary jar (equally spaced apart from one another).

❖ Place ½ cup pillar of bliss wax into 6 ziplock bags (that is ½ cup wax in each bag).

❖ Add 1 drop of liquid candle dye to each of these ziplock bags (each bag will be 1 color only, do not mix the colors). When you are done with this step, you should have 6 bags of wax, red, yellow, orange, green, blue, purple. Collect 1 oz. bottle of rainbow fragrance oil and equally share it with all 6 bags of wax. Mix well.

❖ One bag at a time, place the colored, scented wax into your jar, creating a layered rainbow. Keep your wicks straight and spaced correctly in the jar. Trim wicks.

❖ Enjoy.

# Rustic Wax Melt Candle

[109]

## Ingredients

1. christmas wassail fragrance oil

2. juniper berries whole

3. orange peel cut and sifted

4. 2 ¾ inch cinnamon sticks

5. 10 pounds pillar of bliss wax

6. cloves whole

7. 24 brownie bites silicone soap mold

8. pouring pot

9. thermometer

## Instructions

❖ Prepare herbs. You will need about an ounce of each juniper berries, orange peel and whole cloves. Place them together in a bowl and mix them together.

❖ Melt your pillar of bliss candle wax. You will need about 345g candle wax, when wax reaches a temperature of about 180OF, add 41g christmas wassail fragrance oil. Stir the wax to fully incorporate your fragrance oil.

❖ Before you pour your candle wax, you will want to add the herbs to each cavity of the mold. So, fill each cavity with a small amount of the herbs you prepared in step one.

[110]

❖ Topping each wax tart with a cinnamon stick, we will need a total of 24 pieces of the cinnamon sticks. Simply break each stick into 2 – 3 pieces and place them near your mold.

❖ Finally fill each cavity of your mold with the melted pillar of bliss. Then, top each cavity with a cinnamon stick. Once wax melts have set up, remove them from the mold.

❖ Once you have allowed your rustic melts to cure for a couple of days they are ready to use. Simply place a wax melt in your wax burner and enjoy

# Don Beeswax Candle

[112]

# Ingredients

1. 3 – 5 pounds 100 % pure beeswax

2. wick

3. Deep container such as a metal tin or glass jar

4. water

5. wax paper

# Instructions

❖ Chop beeswax into large pieces. Place into deep container (I used a glass gallon jar). Over medium heat, heat up a large stockpot full of water.

❖ Place the deep container into the large stockpot. This creates a double-boiler of sorts and allows the beeswax to gently melt in the heat of the water.

❖ Cut a piece of wick to double your desired length. For example, I wanted 6 – 8 inch taper candles so I cut a 16 inch piece of wick. Both ends of the wick will be dipped into the beeswax and you can easily hold it up by the middle.

❖ Once the beeswax is melted, pinch the wick in the middle and let the ends of the wick hang down. Slowly dip the ends into the wax. Dip into a bowl of water (this will 'set' the wax). Shake any excess water off and dip once again into the wax. Repeat the water wax dipping cycle until the candle reaches desired thickness (our tapers were about ¾ inch – 1inch thick).

[113]

❖ Cut the bottom inch of the candle off to create a straight bottom. Dip once more for good measure.

❖ Hang or lay on wax paper to dry. Allow to set for about 24 hours before burning.

# Cake Scented Funfetti Candle

[115]

## Ingredients

1. 2 pint sized (16oz) mason jars

2. hot glue gun

3. 2 – 3 tablespoons water

4. pre waxed wicks

5. 1 – 2 tablespoons corn syrup

6. small paintbrush or cloth

7. ½ cup rainbow jimmies (or similar colorful sprinkles)

8. 1 pound soy wax cubes

9. cupcake scented wax cubes

10. Pencils, pens, or something similar to hold the wicks in place

11. measuring cup with a spout

## Instructions

❖ Use a hot glue gun to attach a wick to the bottom of the jar.

❖ Collect and mix together corn syrup and water in a separate bowl, and coat the inside of the Mason jar with the mixture. A small paintbrush can help you reach the lower parts.

[116]

- ❖ While holding the jar horizontally, add a spoonful of sprinkles, and slowly roll the jar around to mix them up inside. Add another spoonful and repeat until the jar is covered completely.

- ❖ Lay a pen or pencil across the tops of the jars and tape the wicks to them to keep the wicks centered.

- ❖ Heat to melt 3 or 4 of the scent cubes wax using a double boiler, or a makeshift one with a pot and heat proof bowl (you can fill a pot half full with water, bring to a simmer, and set a metal bowl on top).

- ❖ Once melt, pour 2 cups of melted wax into a measuring cup with a spout. Leave the rest of the melted wax in the bowl over simmering water. Then slowly pour the wax into the jar. Try to pour it directly into the center and away from the sides.

- ❖ Freeze for about 3 – 4 hours or until the wax has firmed up, and then your funfetti candle is ready to use

# French Vanilla Candle

## Ingredients

1. Candle wick

2. Candle wax

3. Coffee beans

4. Vanilla beans, chopped

## Instructions

❖ Heat wax to boil using a double boiler or a microwave safe bowl. Glue the wick in place at the bottom of the cup or just hold it in place with your hand (at the top, of course).

❖ Pour in a small layer of wax and add a layer of coffee beans and vanilla beans. Then fill the rest of the cup with wax. You can stir the wax with a disposable chopstick to distribute the beans if needed.

❖ Allow the wax solidify for about 16 – 14 hours and trim the wick

# Chunky Votive Candle

# Ingredients

1. 1 oz essential oil or essential oil blend

2. 1.5 lb. soy candle wax

3. tabbed wicks (with metal bottom)

4. soap/candle thermometer

5. wooden stick for stirring

# Instructions

❖ Collect 1.5 lbs of wax into your pour pot, place the pour pot in a saucepan filled 1/3 of the way with water and allow to boil. Stir the wax with a wooden stick or chopstick until the wax melts completely. The melting point of soy wax is generally 125OF. The final temperature of fully melted wax may be upwards of 160 – 180OF. When wax is melted, measure the temperature of the wax with the thermometer. You will need the melted wax to cool a bit before you reach the best pour temperature range of 110 – 140OF.

❖ Add, add 1 oz essential oil, wwhen it reach pour temperature, stir once to incorporate wax and pour wax into the containers. I have come across recommendations to heat the containers first with a hair dryer and my assumption is that this may prevent cracking in case the wax is far hotter than the container can handle. I have never had a problem with this, though, and usually skip this step, particularly with aluminum tins.

[121]

- ❖ Containers such as thick, heat proof glass, aluminum tins, tea cups, ceramic containers, etc

- ❖ Once all the wax is poured, quickly insert the tabbed wick into the center. Allow candles to cool for several hours and then trim the wicks and feel free to use.

# Coffee Bean Soy Candle

[123]

# Ingredients

1. glass measuring cup

2. 2 cups soy wax

3. 1 8 oz mason jar

4. 1 candlewick (with a weighted bottom)

5. candle thermometer

6. ½ teaspoon vanilla candle scent

7. pencil

8. scissors

9. 15 whole coffee beans

10. ½ teaspoon coffee grounds

# Instructions

❖ Collect 2 cups soy wax to a large glass measuring cup (do not use a plastic measuring cup), heat in a microwave for about 2 – 3 minutes, stirring every 30 seconds

❖ Stir your wax until the temperate reaches 167OF on a candle thermometer.

❖ Mix in the vanilla scent and stir well to incorporate. Place 6 – 7 whole coffee beans in the bottom of the Mason jar along with a pinch of coffee grounds.

[124]

❖ Dip your candle wick into the melted wax. Place your wax dipped candlewick in a Mason jar allowing the bottom of the wick to drop to

❖ the bottom of the jar.

❖ To hold the candlewick in place, wrap the top around a pencil or chopstick or skewer. Place the pencil (chopstick or skewer) over the jar and let the bottom of it drop to the bottom. A weighted candlewick does this nicely and settles on its own.

# Sinus Relief Candle

[126]

# Ingredients

1. 4 – 8 ounce size glass jar

2. 15 drops pure eucalyptus essential oil

3. 12 drops rosemary essential oil,

4. 10 drops pure lemon essential oil

5. 1 brick paraffin wax (preformulated)

6. 15 drops peppermint essential oil

7. 1 candlewick  (with a weighted bottom)

8. wax adhesive (if desired)

9. thermometer

# Instructions

❖ Fill the bottom half of a double boiler to about one third full and over a medium high heat. Place wax brick in the top half and allow to melt. This type of paraffin wax is preformulated and will melt easily. You should not need to stir it more than once or twice until you are adding the oils. Do not overheat the wax, so keep a close watch on the water in the bottom pot and once it begins to boil, just turn reduce to low heat. The melting timeis between 10 – 12 minutes.

❖ Attach the wick to the bottom of the glass jar so it is all ready to go when the wax is ready to pour. You have two options for this: Either use wax adhesive, which is sold in the craft store near the paraffin wax, or you can place a few drops of the hot wax from the pan into the bottom of your jar and set the clip down in it, holding it in place for a few seconds to secure it on. (You can do the pencil trick to hold it in place, and readjust after you pour your wax mixture, or use a ruler and clothes pin. Loop the wick around the pencil or ruler to hold it in place.)

❖ Once wax has melted and is nice and clear in color, check the temperature with a thermometor to see if it is good, as per the directions listed on the package. It may need to cool a bit before adding the essential oils.

❖ Add in your essential oils to the melted wax and stir. Pour the wax mixture into the jar, until it is approximately ¾ full. You will need more wax later to top off the candle, so reserve some (keep it from the heat, and just turn off the heat for now).

❖ Adjust your wick if it moved from center. Allow candle to cool for about 20 minutes and using a sharp object poke a hole a few times in the wax, (I used the end of my thermometer), close to the wick itself, to remove the trapped air that gets in when you fill it.

❖ Reheat the reserved wax over medium heat and when it has reached the right temperature again, pour it over the holes in the top of the candle, filling them in and topping the rest of the candle off till the jar is full.

Made in the USA
Monee, IL
15 May 2022

96449289R00074